IMAGES OF ENGLAND

AROUND
THORNBURY
REVISITED

IMAGES OF ENGLAND

AROUND
THORNBURY
REVISITED

MEG WISE

TEMPUS

*This book is dedicated to Tom Crowe
(1935-2004). All royalties are going to
Thornbury and District Heritage Trust.*

Frontispiece: Frank Taylor (left) and Clifford Messenger, two of
the ushers at the Thornbury Picture House on the High Street,
are seen here in their smart uniforms and highly polished shoes
in 1935.

First published 2006

Tempus Publishing Limited
The Mill, Brimscombe Port,
Stroud, Gloucestershire, GL5 2QG
www.tempus-publishing.com

British Library Cataloguing in Publication Data.
A catalogue record for this book is available from the British Library.

ISBN 0 7524 3761 5

Typesetting and origination by Tempus Publishing Limited.
Printed in Great Britain.

Contents

Acknowledgements

The author wishes to thank all those people, too numerous to mention by name, who offered photographs, information and encouragement for this book, and for their sympathy and patience following the sad death of Tom Crowe in 2004. Special thanks to the following people and organisations for their invaluable assistance: Rosemary Cave, Rita Crowe, Mike Edwards, Jean and Martin Elton, George Ford, Eric Garrett, Gazette Newspapers, Roger Hall, Margaret and Derek Hawkins, Miss J.D. Higgins, Roger Howell, Bob Jordan, Allan Knapp, Pam Lewis, Heather Palmer, Diana Ross, Sandi Shallcross, Mike Tozer, Colin, Graeme and Ian Wise, Ken Worsley, and colleagues at Thornbury and District Museum and in the Research Group.

The Trust has endeavoured to locate the origins of all the pictures in this book and to seek permission for their reproduction. We apologise to anyone we have missed in this search and hope that we have not given offence. For many of the names given in the captions we have had to rely on the memories of contributors and inevitably there will be some mistakes. We apologise to anyone affected by this and ask that you contact us so that we can correct our records.

To contact the Trust please write to:

Thornbury and District Heritage Trust
Town Hall
35 High Street
Thornbury
BS35 2AR

Or via e-mail to: enquiries@thornburymuseum.org

Introduction

This book follows on from the success of *Around Thornbury* which was compiled by Tom Crowe, Chairman of Thornbury and District Heritage Trust, and published in 2003. Tom had already started work on a second book when he died suddenly on 9 April 2004. The Trust resolved to finish the book in his memory and believes it is a fitting tribute to a man who gave so much inspiration to others.

As before, the book covers not only the villages close to Thornbury but also more distant places like Charfield and Pilning; this is because Thornbury Museum's collecting area covers the western part of the Unitary Authority of South Gloucestershire, some fourteen parishes in total.

Thornbury, as the largest place, is dealt with first. Then the surrounding villages are presented in alphabetical order, and the space allocated to each reflects the amount or quality of material available. We hope that the information provided in the captions will add to people's knowledge of the area. The Research Group, founded by Tom Crowe, continues to thrive and members have been very helpful in compiling the captions. This group is open to anyone who is interested in finding out more about the local history of Thornbury and the surrounding district.

To accompany Chapter Three, a short history of Thornbury Grammar School, based on works by B. Stafford Morse and L.G. Taylor, has been included at the end of this introduction, to celebrate the school's 400th anniversary in 2006.

The earliest evidence of occupation in the area dates back to the Neolithic Age and by the time of Domesday, Thornbury was an important and wealthy manor. Until the last few decades the district's economy was based largely on agriculture and the trades that supported it. In the Severn Vale, this took the form of dairy farming with more arable farms on the higher ground to the east. Salmon farming was carried out from Aust to the northern limit of our district but is no longer in operation. Other industries have also disappeared. There used to be coal mining at Rangeworthy, brick making at Littleton, Cattybrook and Oldbury-on-Severn; Thornbury had a brick works as well as a sawmill and once used to produce its own gas and electricity. Quarrying used to be carried out at Alveston and Cromhall and still continues at Tytherington.

Thornbury and District Heritage Trust have operated a museum in Chapel Street since 1986. This houses both document and photographic archives and a collection of artefacts relating to the history of the area. Several exhibitions are produced each year and the museum is run entirely voluntarily.

Thornbury Grammar School, 1606-2006

The history of the Grammar School can be traced back to two earlier schools. The first dates from 1606, in which year John Jones 'gave a House & Garden in the Borough of Thornbury towards a Free School to be called the Free School of Thornbury'. In 1642, William White gave the school property and land, followed by a similar gift in 1648 by William Edwards. It is known that by this date a small school had been established in premises on the west side of Castle Street, between Kington Lane and the church. This school became known as The Free Grammar School and its buildings still stand. The poor, for whom this sort of free school was provided, were not the labouring poor but the relatively poor; sons of gentry and yeomen who were likely to become clergymen or take up other professions. The curriculum would probably have been based on Latin, with Greek being taught to the older pupils. An advertisement for the school in March 1869 gives the fees as ten guineas per annum for 'the usual Classical Course' and six guineas for 'those requiring an English Education to fit them for Business Pursuits'.

The second school was founded in 1729 when Mr John Attwells 'gave £500 in trust to Feoffees, to purchase Lands wherewith to endow a Free School for the Instruction of poor Boys and poor Girls of the Town of Thornbury, being Parishioners there, in Reading, Writing, Arithmetic, Sewing and Knitting'. This school was set up in a house in St Mary Street and was known as The Free School or Attwells School. At his own expense, Mr Kingsmill Grove added 'a commodious schoolroom' adjoining the rear of the house around 1811. The school building later became a church institute and still exists, being known until recently as the Compleat Cookshop.

In 1869 a government inspector examined these two schools; his report was highly critical of both so a plan was developed by the Charity Commissioners to merge both schools into one. In 1879 the Thornbury Grammar School was founded and Mr George Nixon was appointed headmaster. Land in Gloucester Road was purchased for the new school and the first building opened in 1880. To this was added a house for the headmaster and then, as numbers increased, other buildings in 1906, 1909 and 1932. The school motto *Disce aut Discede* means 'Learn or Leave'. The rest of the phrase *Tertia sors manet – vapula!* ('There remains a third choice – the stick!',) was omitted.

With the coming of comprehensive schools in the 1960s, the school eventually lost its grammar school status. A new school, Marlwood, was built in Alveston, and the grammar school's activities transferred there in 1972. The Gloucester Road site was handed over to the Castle School, and today it is the Castle School's sixth-form centre.

Meg Wise
December 2005

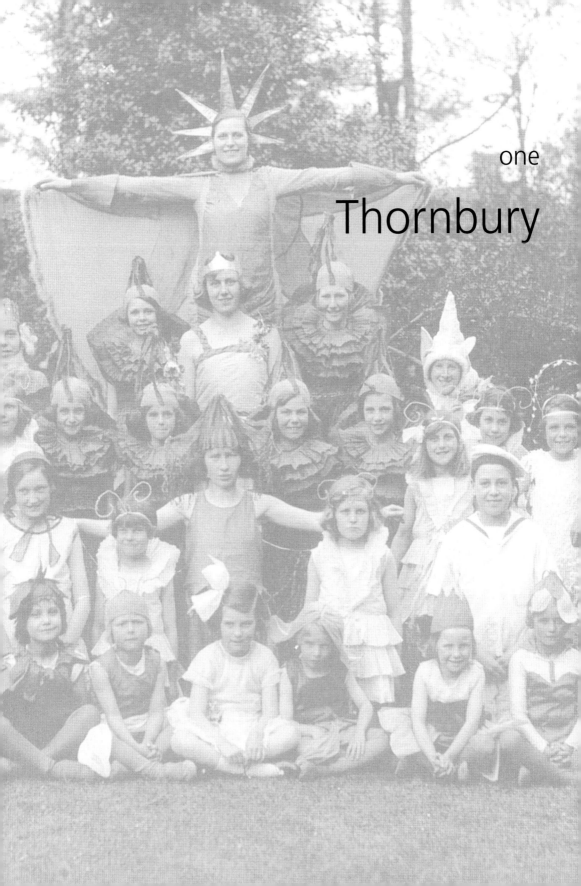

one

Thornbury

Left: The beautiful tower of the parish church of St Mary the Virgin is seen here in 1889 with scaffolding erected to rebuild the pinnacles that had become unsafe. Supervised by Mr Waller, architect to Gloucester Cathedral, the work was carried out by Thornbury mason Frank Kelson Howell. It was completed at a cost of nearly £1,000, using much of the original stone and keeping to the original sixteenth–century design.

Below: A television camera, lighting and microphone can be seen inside St Mary's church when it played host to the popular BBC programme *Songs of Praise* on 18 January 1967.

Above: Members of the Howard family outside Thornbury Castle, *c.* 1872. The needs of early photography required the picture to be staged to avoid blurring; close examination reveals that the leading velocipedes are propped up. From left to right: Esme William Howard, Lady Gwendoline Herbert, Edward Stafford Howard, Henry Charles Howard of Greystoke and Thornbury.

Right: In the gardens of Thornbury Castle are, from left to right: Revd Canon Robert G. Rawstorne, vicar of Thornbury 1943 to 1976, John P. Fane de Salis of Fairfield House in Castle Street and S.J.V. Rouch, headmaster of Thornbury Grammar School. The vicar is keeping a close eye on Barney, a dog that was known to be fond of nipping ankles!

Above: Thornbury vicarage, photographed by G. Courtenay Chambers a week before the building was partially destroyed by fire in August 1894. The vicar at the time was Revd Henry B. Hodgson. Born in Thornbury, his son, Lt William Noel Hodgson MC, was a war poet and wrote his last poem, *Before Action,* on the eve of the Battle of the Somme. He was killed in action the next day, 1 July 1916, aged twenty-three.

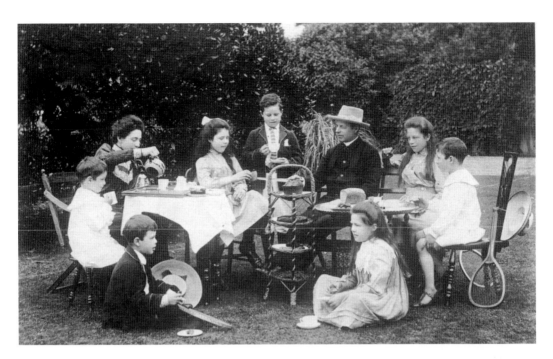

Above: Reverend Canon Cornwall and his wife, Alice Louisa (*née* Cripps), taking afternoon tea on the vicarage lawn with their seven children, *c.* 1908. Canon Cornwall was vicar of Thornbury from 1899 to 1924. The children are (eldest first): Isabel, Alice, Frances, Alan, John, Richard and Nigel. Note the wooden tennis rackets.

Right: John Oates DCM, RSM, Somerset Light Infantry, with his wife Eliza (*née* Fowler), *c.* 1901. Having fought in the Boer War, John Oates trained men at Aldershot during the Great War. He was a lay preacher and as a parish councillor he fought for the fair allocation of the almshouses and for the provision of the first public toilets in Thornbury.

Opposite below: Following the fire, a new vicarage was built on the same site by Mr J.B. Hudson of Yate from plans prepared by Mr Frederick Waller of Gloucester. It was dedicated on Saturday 16 November 1895 by the Right Revd Bishop Marsden when a choral service was held in the drawing room. The building recently became a private house.

Above: Pupils of the Sheiling Curative school playing in the gardens to the rear of Thornbury House in the 1950s, when part of the school occupied the building.

Left: Thornbury House was built shortly before 1811 by Kingsmill Grove, who owned a papermaking and stationery business in Bristol. In the 1880s it was the home of Maj. Gen. Pierrepont Mundy and his second wife Geraldine, daughter of Revd Maurice Fitzgerald Townsend Stephens, vicar of Thornbury from 1828 to 1872. The house was pulled down in the 1970s, and was replaced by the houses of Warwick Place.

Opposite below: Pupils attending the official opening in the hall of the Castle School. The white shirts and navy blue, grey and gold-striped ties have only recently been abandoned in favour of modern polo shirts with the school crest.

Above: After many years of overcrowding at the County Secondary School at Gillingstool, the Castle School in Park Road was officially opened on 19 November 1966. From left to right: Mr Rendall, the headmaster of Thornbury Grammar School, the Duke of Beaufort, the Bishop of Gloucester, Revd Canon Rawstorne, Mr C.J. Martin (headmaster of the Castle School), Mr Hugh Wells (the Chair of Governors).

Above: Children at the Church of England National School photographed for a presentation certificate marking the retirement of the headteachers in 1905. The original school, dating back to before 1839, was a modest building just to the east of St Mary's church. A new building across the road was completed in 1862 at a cost of £831. This school is now known as St Mary's Church of England Primary School. There are only a few known pictures of the school or its pupils before the 1960s.

Left: In 1866, Thomas Golding and Fanny Fill were appointed Master and Mistress of the new school and were to remain in charge for almost thirty-nine years. They lived next door in School House and some of their children went on to become teachers in Thornbury. It is believed this picture was taken at their retirement in 1905.

Opposite below: Miss Chell's class at the Church of England School, 1954. From left to right, back row: -?- , Brian Nicholls, -?-, -?-, Terry Griffiths, -?-, Alan Webb. Middle row: -?-, -?-, -?-, -?-, Malcolm Longman, -?-, -?-, -?-, Andrew Rawstorne, -?-. Front row: -?-, Elizabeth Ball, -?-, -?-, -?-, Yvonne Billett, -?-, Jilly Bennett, -?-.

Above: The headmaster of the Church of England School, Mr Samuel William Gallop Dennis, with the children of Form III, *c.* 1931. From left to right, back row: George Lugg, Lillian Benjamin, Edith Moorman, Ronnie Gough, Wilfred Pearce, Ronnie Symes, Mary Wilkes, Joan Barge. Middle row: Mary Lambert, Connie Sellars, Kathleen Skinner, Iris Always, Vera Wilkes, Edith Millen. Front row: Ivy Wilkes, Hetty Reeves, Ruth Child, Joyce Shipp, Lucy Shipp.

Above: Processions often thronged the main streets of Thornbury. Congregating round the pump on the Plain, around 1900, are members of the Rational Sick and Burial Association on their fête day, held on the first Monday in June. This association was one of the Friendly Societies that through weekly meetings and subscriptions offered its members sickness and burial benefit paid out of the pool of savings that built up. Note that nearly everyone is wearing a hat.

Below: Part of the Thornbury Carnival held in May 1937 to celebrate the coronation of King George VI; the setting is a field at the castle lent for the occasion by Major Algar Howard. The sign on the vehicle on the left of the picture reads 'BBC Chamber Music' and several chamber pots are visible! It is not known whether the policeman is in fancy dress or not.

Above: Entries for parades gathered at the railway station before processing through the town. As part of the Silver Jubilee parade in 1935, 'The Roosters' featured butcher Harry Trayhurn playing the fiddle, with his son, Don Trayhurn, standing at the rear of the cart. Immediately behind Mr Trayhurn are, from left to right: Harry Phillips (in the top hat), –?–, Howard Lewis, Arthur C. Lewis. The coachman is W. Bennett. Even the horse wanted to be in the picture!

Below: The celebrations for the Silver Jubilee of King George V and his consort Queen Mary were held in Thornbury on 6 May 1935. Behind the band is St George and the Dragon, a tableau designed by Mrs F.H. Grace. The Jubilee Queen was Miss Edna Coles.

Above: The Parish Council Fire Brigade was in full operation by December 1899. This magnificent scene at Thornbury Castle is thought to date from 1900 when E. Stafford Howard donated a six-man manual engine to enable the brigade to pump water more effectively. Carrying the hose reel, centre right, is blacksmith Oliver Higgins. Second from the right is High Street draper Arthur H. Wilkins, who was the first captain, a position he held until 1938.

Right: Thornbury doctor Edward Mills Grace (1841 to 1911), the elder brother of W.G. Grace, was also an outstanding all round cricketer playing for Gloucester and England. Cricket may have been played before his arrival in the town but it was E.M. Grace who established a thriving cricket club in the early 1870s, moving the matches to a new, larger ground beside the Ship Inn at Alveston in 1872.

Below: Situated behind Wilding's store on the High Street, Park House was for many years the home of Dr E.M. Grace. On his death in 1911 it was purchased for £1,400 by local solicitor H.P. Thurston. Several years later Dr Grace's son, Dr Edgar Mervyn Grace, bought Park House and ran his general practice from it.

Opposite below: The old fire station, built in 1930, on the High Street, *c.* 1947. The fountain on the wall, between the engines, had been erected on this site in 1880 to commemorate Lt Hector Maclaine of the Royal Horse Artillery who was murdered after being taken prisoner during the Battle of Maiwand; it was later moved to a wall at the top of Castle Street. A new fire station on the Gloucester Road came into operation in 1980.

Above: Thornbury Baptists on an outing to Weston-super-Mare, *c.* 1933. From left to right, back row: Sidney Dearing, Mervyn Carver, -?-, -?-. Second row: Church Elder George Stone, Revd W. West Johnson (minister from 1928 to 1933), Mrs Johnson, Arthur C. Lewis, Mrs A.C. Lewis, Deacon and choirmaster Harry Philips, Irene Northover, -?-, Arthur Walker. Third row: Mrs Len Smith, Mrs Taylor, Frances Carver, Mrs A. Walker. Kneeling: Frances Taylor, Mons Smith. Sitting: Ron Lewis, Len Taylor.

Left: The Pastor and Deacons of Thornbury Baptist church, *c.* 1905. Sitting on the right is Pastor William Walter Reed. Standing behind him is George Stone, who was a carpenter at Thornbury Castle; he became a member of the church in 1872 and later became an Elder and Deacon.

Opposite above: Pupils of the preparatory school, run by Mrs Lucy Chambers at Rosemount House on the High Street, *c.* 1895. Mr John Taylor Chambers taught organ, piano and violin; he was also the organist at St Mary's church from 1864 until his death in 1924. Their daughter, Beatrice Chambers, is standing in the centre in the back row.

Opposite below: Pupils at Miss Mabel Ellen Trayhurn's preparatory school, situated on the High Street where Hawkin's hardware shop now stands, *c.* 1937. An advertisement from 1940 reads 'Spacious and airy school rooms of modern type. Aim – to provide thorough training in the groundwork which is so necessary in preparing children in their later education. Backward and delicate children receive special attention without undue pressure. Extra subjects pianoforte and dancing'.

Members of the congregation of the Wesley chapel on the High Street gathered in their Sunday best for the opening of a schoolroom at the rear of the building in 1907. The church was opened around 1878. Note the ornate gas lamps and walls that were later removed from what is now known as the Methodist church.

The same group pictured behind the church by the schoolroom. This building had originally been erected at the Hackett in 1894 as the Church of England 'iron' Mission Church of St Paul, but was replaced by the present stone church in 1905.

Above: The Picture House was on the High Street where Besley Hill Estate Agents and Park Insurance Services now stand. Provided by Edmund Cullimore, his daughter Mrs Helen Grace ran it, followed by her daughter Mrs Ruth Rowe until it closed in 1959. Officially opened on 1 May 1920 by Canon Cornwall, with a special showing of *The Nature of the Beast*, a silent film directed by Cecil M. Hepworth, the films advertised in the Picture House window suggest a date of around 1945.

Left: The front of the programme for the pantomime *Jack and the Beanstalk* staged at the Picture House in 1938. Mrs Helen Grace started producing pantomimes in the cinema in 1936. The whole family was involved; members of the wider community and especially many local children loved to take part in these well-rehearsed and elaborate productions.

"Jack and the Beanstalk"

— THE CAST —

JACK	ELIZABETH GRACE	GIANT'S WIFE	EDNA BARTLETT
MRS. GRUBBLE	BILLY POOLE	FAIRY BEANFLOWER	JOAN HAMILTON
PRINCESS TRUELOVE	PHYLLIS BEAVEN	DEMON DISCORD	FRED SAINSBURY
BARONESS DE BROKE	BARBARA BRUTON	TIM	FRED BENNETT
BARON DE BROKE	CHARLIE POOLE	TOM	REGGIE TAYLOR
GIANT GORRIBUSTER	DOUGLAS GARN	CUCKOO (a Cow)	

VILLAGERS—S. Brealy, W. Hill, M. Hill, V. Longman, N. Oates, A. Poole, N. Pullen, J. Pullen.

SPECIALITY DANCERS—Marguerite and Ruth Grace.

Pianist—E. MASON, F.R.C.O.

Drummer—G. EXCELL.

Costumes made by MISS N. HUGHES.

SNOWBALL & PONY DANCE—M. Councell, J. Dearing, C. Dearing, N. Exell, R. Ford, J. Gough, M. Gough, A. Higgins, E. Longman, D. Smith.

FAIRIES—J. Cook, I. Holpin, J. Perry, M. Payne, D. Rugman, C. Shepherd.

IMPS—J. Councell, G. Collins, J. Ford, P. Holpin, P. Rogers, J. Rugman.

SCENES.

Scene 1—Outside the Giant's Castle.
Scene 2—Outside Mother Grubble's Cottage.
Scene 3—The Market Place.
Scene 4—The Fairy Glen.

INTERVAL.

Scene 5—Inside Mother Grubble's Cottage.
Scene 6—The Beanstalk.
Scene 7—Cloudland.
Scene 8—Inside the Giant's Castle.
Scene 9—Outside Mother Grubble's Cottage.
Scene 10—Finale.

Above: Centre pages from the programme that also contained an outline of the plot, set in make-believe Thornybru town: 'The fearsome Giant Gorribuster, a menace to the peace-loving inhabitants of Thornybru, is in love with the beautiful Princess Truelove, to marry whom he declares he would give his soul. When the wicked Demon Discord hears of this he agrees to strike a bargain; in exchange for the giant's soul he promises to assist him in winning the hand of the Princess'.

Opposite below: The cast of *Jack and the Beanstalk. The Gazette* of 26 February 1938 reported that 'the delightful dancing, catchy choruses, clever comedy combined with gay costumes and lavish settings made it a production which provided enjoyment for all who saw it'.

Right: Elizabeth Grace as Jack being menaced by Douglas Garn as Giant Gorribuster. Miss Sally Grace designed the scenery and Miss Nellie Hughes made the costumes. Douglas Garn died while serving as a sergeant in the RAF during the Second World War.

Below: The girls who performed the Snowball Dance in *Jack and the Beanstalk* in 1938. From left to right, back row: Ellen Longman, Rita Ford. Second row: Amy Higgins, Mary Gough. Third row: Joan Dearing, Cynthia Dearing. Fourth row: Mary Councell, Nellie Exell. Front row: Joyce Gough, Doreen Smith.

Left: The Yate to Thornbury branch line was opened by the Midland Railway Co. in 1872, causing much celebration in the town. The first stationmaster was Mr James Brant followed, from around 1899, by Mr Charles Radcliffe Cooper (left) who retired in 1921 after fifty-two years of railway service; he died in 1945 at the age of ninety. On the right is believed to be his son, Phillip Cooper, who became the third stationmaster.

Below: The MR insignia on the men's hats indicates that this photograph of Thornbury station was probably taken just before the Midland Railway became part of the London, Midland & Scottish Railway in 1923. From left to right, back row: Bill Whiteman, James Biddle Hill, -?-, Alfred Gill, -?-, guard George Nicholls, Bill Short, -?-, -?-, coal merchant Alfred Davis. Middle row: George Clutterbuck, -?-, -?-, -?-, Phillip Cooper, Charles Cooper, -?-, -?-. Front row (seated): -?-, -?-.

Opposite above: Driver Bill Short beside a locomotive at Thornbury station, sometime in the 1930s. The site of the station spanned approximately the area either side of, and including, what is now Midland Way from its junction with the Bristol Road to a little past its junction with Rock Street. Some of the boundary walls of the station can still be seen today.

The last passenger train ran in June 1944, although hospital trains used the station during the latter stages of the war, when casualties were taken to the military hospital at Tortworth Court. A freight service continued until the mid-1960s. Staff at the station in 1944 were, from left to right: driver Jim Whiteman, fireman Sam Taylor, porter S. Collins, drayman Arthur Knapp, stationmaster Mr Hamer, ganger Dick Travel, guard Bert Millen, tun porter Graham Lock, ganger Jim Hill, plate layer G. Clutterbuck.

Left: Robert Withers (1866–1924) stands on the right with his young son, Charles, outside his premises on the west side at the top of the High Street, *c.* 1905. The sign above the door reads 'Brougham, Waggonette, Traps & Saddle Horses Let On Hire. Orders Taken Here. Good Stabling In St Mary's Street'. This building is currently a dental practice.

Below: Edmund Cullimore had interests in the Gas Light & Coke Co. and the Thornbury & District Electricity Co. Ltd; both were operated by his son-in-law Francis Henry Grace. The showrooms were on St John Street where Adrian Hair and Beauty salon now stands.

Above: This gentleman is believed to be Joseph Ogborn, who came to Thornbury to run the butcher's shop on the High Street (now the Mogul Shamrat restaurant) when his father, John, died in 1881. By 1906, Matilda Ogborn was in charge of the business. Events like fairs and sports matches took place on the land behind the premises, known as Ogborn's field.

Right: Inside the Swan Inn on the High Street in the early 1930s are, from left to right: the landlord of the Swan, Mr Ernest Herbert Theophilus, Paul Organ, (landlord of the White Hart at Olveston) and Mr John Evomy Phelps. Mr Phelps was known to many as Dr Phelps, but he was actually a surgeon's assistant working for Dr Grace; he was also the Deputy Registrar for births and deaths.

Left: Thomas Ball's premises, known as Empire House, in Silver Street in the 1920s. The family removed to Cheltenham but returned to the area to farm at Siblands. Motor engineer Tommy H. Ashcroft was running his car, motorcycle and cycle business here in the 1940s.

Below: The Horseshoe Inn at the corner of St Mary Street and Horseshoe Lane in the early 1900s. These buildings, near to the library, now house the Charcoal Grill and Giggs Hair and Beauty salon.

Opposite above: The children of Thornbury Council School were treated to a special tea party to celebrate Queen Victoria's Diamond Jubilee in 1897. Note the china cups and saucers, and also that the boys and girls are seated at separate tables.

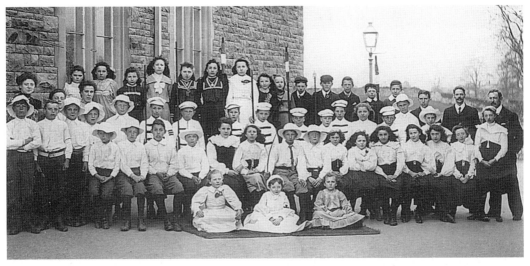

Children at the Council School, *c.* 1905. From left to right, back row: Beatrice Clutterbuck, Dorothy Cripps, Mabel Baylis, Julia Riddiford, ? Ponting, -?-, Doreen Underhill, May Horsman, E. Phillips, I. Longden, E. Davis, C. Cripps, A. Dixon, R. Baylis. Second row, teachers: Miss Horner, Miss Agnes Ann, Miss Mabel Cooper, Mr Alfred Burchell, Mr Ralph Bolton, headmaster Mr F.H. Cresswell. Third row: Arthur Allsopp, Dennis Beazant, Percy Baylis, Harold Higgins, William Carter, George Ford, -?-, Rodney Horsman, Richard Anstey, Howard Baylis, Victor Yarnold, William Allsopp, Beatrice Ponting, Harold Mosdale, Bert Dayman, B. Phillips. Fourth row: Elton English, Harry Bannister, Gerald Fudge, William Gill, Lydia Riddiford, -?-, Percy Horsman, Cecil Symes, Nellie Simms, Bertha Stone, Emily Cripps, -?-, -?-, Dorothy Symes, Lily Reeves (standing). Front row: Hetty Carter, N. Eddington, L. Howse.

Left: Mr W.H. Nicholls was headmaster of the Council School (now Gillingstool primary) from 1927 to 1961, overseeing many changes including the setting up of a secondary school on the site. From 1935 he also ran a successful Evening Institute and from 1945, with the setting up of a youth centre in the school grounds, he was the Youth Leader and Secretary to the District Youth Committee.

Below: A class at the Council School, *c.* 1929. Judging from the footwear of all but one girl in the front row, long lace-up boots were a must. From left to right, back row: Hubert Spill, Don Pearce, Eric Williams, Norman Pearce, Percy Vizzard, Don Trayhurn, Major Webb. Middle row: Lily Pitman, Nellie Pullen, Joan Davis, Nora Oates, Vincent Oates, Desmond Wyatt, Don Adams, Ron Davis. Front row: Rachael Phillips, Joan Livall, Beatrice Hill, Irene State, Iris Long, Vera Davis, Poppy Watkins.

Opposite above: A class at the Council School, *c.* 1928. From left to right, back row: Tony Billett, Lionel Pearce, John King, Flossie Parker, ? Parker, Brenda Skuse, George Skuse. Middle row: Roy Billett, ? Pearce, Norman King, Winifred Hill, ? Payne, Frank Taylor, Amy Poole, Joan Dearing. Front row: Josie Billett, Joan King, Ruby Hill, (possibly) George Payne, ? Taylor, Ken Poole, Cynthia Dearing.

Miss Tonkin's class at the Council School in 1938. From left to right, back row: Brian Smith, Des Holpin, Jeff Screen, -?-, Tony Sherman, Ben Salisbury, -?-, John Withers, -?-, George Hardy, Gilbert Roberts, John Pridham. Middle row: Philip Hacker, Doug Messenger, Herbert Livall, David Cullimore, Roger Davis, Kath Riddiford, Jill Gazzard, Pam Rodgers, Betty Longman, Mabel Webb, -?-, Ruth Knight, Miss Tonkin. Front row: Bill Skuse, Norm Smith, Derek Harris, Harold King, Cyril Davis, Dorothy Collins, Olive Taylor, Betty Witts, Pearl Peters, Vera Pearce, Alma Davis, Dorothy Clutterbuck.

May 1942 saw the beginnings of the canteen at the Council School that was to supply school meals in the area. By October 1943 almost 500 meals were being delivered daily to the Council School and to the Church of England schools of Thornbury, Oldbury-on-Severn, Alveston and Olveston. Some time around 1945, the canteen staff were, from left to right, back row: Mrs V. Ginn, Mrs V. Vizzard, Kathleen Riddiford, Mrs B. Screen. Front row: Mrs Roberts, canteen supervisor Miss Joan Hook, Irene Strong.

The Council School in 1948. The building on the right was the youth club. From left to right, back row: Jean Jefferies, Mary Stuart, Marjory Driver, Audrey Witts, Mr Fill, Margaret Paxford, Brenda Croxon, Maureen Collins, Shirley Caise, Betty Cosser, Ann Sturgess. Middle row: Ann Bishop, Margaret Hamilton, Valerie Billett, Margaret Hand, Barbara Juggins, Janet Reid, Christine England, Shirley King, Marion Hawker, Barbara Curtis. Front row: Margaret Barton, Pearl Witchard, Sheila Davis, Janet Flight, Elizabeth Pearce, Jean Smith, Shirley Clutterbuck.

Four classrooms were built on the Council School vegetable garden in 1950. In 1951 these formed the nucleus of the County Secondary School that admitted children from around Thornbury, Aust, Pilning and the Almondsbury area. Pupils seen here around 1962 were, from left to right, back row: -?-, -?-, George Howell, Robin Shipp, Jimmy Knapp, David Boyce, ? Taylor, -?-, Christopher Taylor, -?-, -?-. Middle row: -?-, Denise Cousins, Josephine Hughes, Kate Edwards, -?-, Jane Knapp, -?-, Cherie Coots, -?-. Front row: -?-, -?-, -?-, -?-, -?-, David Poole, -?-, Naomi Fisher.

The staff of the County Secondary School, c. 1962. From left to right, back row: Miss Owen, Betty Knapp, Mr Malcolm Scarborough, Mr Norman Ashcroft, Mr Fill, Mr Boreham, -?-, Mrs M. Johnson. Front row: Mr Spencer, -?-, (headmaster) Mr C. Martin, Miss Helen Pitcher, Mr Cudmore.

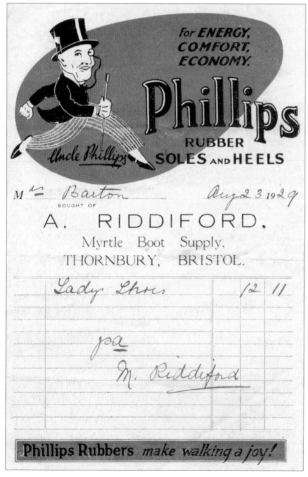

Above: Now demolished, Myrtle Cottage in Horseshoe Lane was once the home of bootmaker Alfred Riddiford JP, clerk to the Parish Council and Burial Board. The sign adjacent to the door indicates he was an agent for Pearl Assurance. He was well known for buying blackberries from people, which he then sold in bulk to Robinson's jam factory in Bristol. Seen here around 1914 are, from left to right, back: Alfred Riddiford, Mrs Minnie Riddiford (*née* Wiltshire). Front: Charlie Riddiford, Harold Riddiford, Winifred Riddiford.

Left: A receipt from Riddiford's shoe shop, known as the Myrtle Boot Supply, dated 1929. People used the 'stick on' Phillips rubber heels and soles to repair leather shoes; the rubber manufacturing company closed in Manchester in 2003 when it relocated much of its production to South Africa.

Right: Views of The Bathings swimming baths are rare. The baths dated back to before 1840 and belonged to the small farm next to them. Thornbury Grammar School children learned to swim here before it closed in the early 1950s. Bill Allsopp, son of policeman Alvin Allsopp, who lived in the police station on the High Street, is ready to take the plunge from the diving board, with Barry Barrington in the background on the high board.

Below: Barry Barrington on the diving board, with his brother-in-law Bill Allsopp in the background, when the Pearce family ran the baths, *c.* 1949. The pool, which was around 6ft deep, was fed by a natural stream running over a filter bed, and as the high surrounding wall kept it in the shade the water was never warm even in the height of summer! The site of the baths is now The Bathings Sheltered Housing.

Castle Street and the Plain on a quiet day sometime before September 1924, when the Rural District Council removed the ornate 1860 pump declaring it a traffic hazard. This resulted in a storm of public protest that included the temporary re-erection of the pump! A replica of the pump was placed in a slightly different position in 1984.

Butcher John Nathaniel Bartlett (left) outside his shop on the Plain, *c.* 1920. This building continued as a butcher's until recently, when it became a dress shop. Next door is James Bevan's boot shop, with a sign in the window advertising cricket boots. Arthur John Bartlett continued his father's business, but from premises next to the Cossham Hall in Chapel Street.

Above: Pullins Green, *c.* 1923. The building with the awning in the distance is Liddiatt and Co., a fishmonger's run by Lucy Liddiatt following the death of her husband Edward in 1898. From 1932 to 1945 it became a grocery shop run by Mr and Mrs A.C. Lewis and later it was Kirby's Fish and Chips. It is now the Hing Tai Fish and Chips and Chinese take away. The nearest building on the right is remembered as Mrs Wall's sweet shop.

Right: Arthur Conway Lewis with sons Ron (right) and John, with Fido the dog, at the rear of the shop on Pullins Green, *c.* 1933. Arthur's wife was Lily Poole; their other children were Nora, Howard and David. Mr Lewis was involved with both the local cricket and football teams and was the organist for Thornbury Baptist church.

The cottages built before 1840 on the left-hand side at the top of Gloucester Road were declared unfit for habitation in the early 1960s. They were pulled down and eventually replaced by the showroom of the garage run by Mr R.H. Shipp.

The garage Richard (Dick) Shipp operated from around 1953 to 1977 at the top of Gloucester Road has since been replaced by housing known as Gloucester Terrace. The Savery family, who still have a shop on the Plain, formerly used the old stone stables at right angles to the road as a garage and engineering works.

Members of the Thornbury pensioners' choir and helpers. From left to right, back row: Ethel Gibson, Mrs Hooper, Mrs Cavanagh, Mrs McGurk, Tricia Biddle, Mrs Bennett, Mrs Cutts, Mrs Brooks, Mrs Iles, Marion Stafford. Behind middle row: Pam Lewis. Middle row: Mrs James, Dolly Scott, Mrs Helen Grace, Joan Exell, -?-, Joan Hawkins. Front row: Mary Coles, Mrs Win Pearce, Joan Bryers.

Members of Thornbury Rural District Council in front of the old workhouse building (now Beechacres) on Gloucester Road, c. 1948. From left to right, back row: S. Cooper, S. Daldry, J. Whelpton, E. Allen, G. Chamberlayne, J. Nichols, J. Pullin, J. Hardwick, R. Iles, F. Ellis, I. Marston. Middle row: J. Hill, C. Williams, F. Kendall, J. Lee, J. King, W. Keen, J. Kitson, F. Mumford, G. Millard, J. Thompson, W. Blair, G. Allen. Front row: H. Booth, Mrs W. Ward, A. Thompson, J. Judd, J. Cooke, F. Lewis, A. Pitcher, H. Stephens, R. Stride.

Left: A portrait of Edmund Cullimore (1850-1941) drawn by his granddaughter, artist Sally Gordon (*née* Grace). Mr Cullimore was the major employer in the town, operating the sawmill and the brickworks (which was situated where Oakleaze Road green is now) as well as having interests in the gas and electricity companies. He was very involved in town affairs being a JP, a Liberal town councillor, a school governor and a lay preacher.

Below: Shen, the house situated just off Gloucester Road, was built in 1891 for Mr Edmund Cullimore as his family home. Later, he had two properties built next to it, West Shen and The Elms, for his adult children to live in.

Above: Staff stir up the Christmas pudding mixture at Thornbury Hospital in the 1950s. P.G. Hawkins & Sons built the hospital section behind the workhouse buildings in the early 1930s and the two wards, Grace and Henderson, were named after two local doctors. From left to right: –?–, –?–, Sister Trotman, Dr E.M. Grace, Matron Ayres, –?–, S.E.N. Hewish.

Right: Edith M. Cotton came to Thornbury at Easter 1947 as a district nurse, and lived in the High Street with a housekeeper named Mrs Fairman. She later moved to Eastbury Close and became a district midwife. She is seen here shortly before her retirement in March 1978 with the last baby she delivered, a boy born at 1.50 a.m. on 9 February, weighing 6lb 4oz.

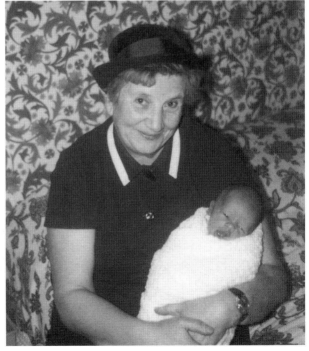

A studio portrait of Dora Beatrice Cullimore, daughter of Luke Cullimore, who was born in Thornbury in 1884. Bicycles were often used as studio props after the cycling craze hit the country in the 1890s.

A wedding group celebrates the marriage of Dora Cullimore to Thomas Ball which took place at St Mary's church on 31 July 1906. The building, Siblands Farm, no longer exists. Sadly Dora died in 1919 leaving four young children; she was a victim of the influenza pandemic which killed more people in the UK than the Great War.

The son of Pullins Green blacksmith Oliver Higgins, Second Lt Claude Wilfred Higgins, married Rhoda at Elmley Castle near Evesham in 1916. From left to right, standing: Harold Higgins, Claude Higgins, Rhoda ?, bride's father. Sitting: Edith Higgins, bride's mother. On 25 April 1917, while serving with the North Staffordshire Regiment, Claude tragically drowned in the River Tigris while attempting to save his friend Frank Harrison.

A more unusual wedding picture was taken on board the Thornbury fire engine on 11 July 1936, after the ceremony had been performed at the Methodist church on the High Street. The groom is fireman Harold 'Pat' Ellis with bride Elsie Louisa Collins of Alveston. Both bridesmaids, Rene Collins (left) and Jean Duncan (right), were nieces of the bride.

The *Capture of Spring* in two acts by Florence Una Norris by permission of publishers Messrs Abel Heywood & Sons Ltd, Manchester, directed by Mrs Helen Grace, was performed at the Picture House on Thursday, Friday and Saturday 1–3 May 1930 as a special attraction to celebrate the tenth anniversary of the opening of the cinema. The cast are seen here, probably in the grounds of Shen or West Shen on Gloucester Road, and the names have been taken from a programme: *King Sun* Miss S. Grace; *Spring* Miss E. Grace; *Winter* Miss N. Hutchins; *Jack Frost* Miss F. Taylor; *Golden Ray (Chief Sunbeam)* Miss P. Hemingway; *Sunbeams* Misses V. Lucas, B. Bruton, E. Garson, P. Poulton, R. Hill and B. Sims; *Ted and Phyllis (Mortal Children)* Misses E. Wakefield and F. Carver; *Flower Fairies* Misses I. State, I. Long, N. Oates, P. Pitman, D. Millin and E. Millin; *Snowflakes* Misses P. Sainsbury, W. Hill, N. Pullen, P. Brealey, M. Grace and R. Grace; *Rag Dolls* P. Sainsbury, M. Grace, R. Grace with Soloist Miss S. Lucas; *Flowers* M. Rogers, H. Poulton, S. Brealey, M. Hill, J. Pullen and E. Longman. *Saturday only* Mr B. Peters and Master E. Grace, *Banjoist*.

Thornbury market was held for many years on the High Street and the Plain until the opening of the New Market site off Rock Street in 1911. This is probably a scene from the opening day and it is assumed that the title 'Selling Pigs at the New Market' refers to an auction going on in the distance as the animals in the foreground are sheep!

A sign advertising Thornbury market in 1969. Following the decline of sales the last livestock market was held on 27 June 1996.

Above: A view that has changed completely is that of Rock Street near the entrance to the market, *c.* 1960. Streamleaze Court has replaced the houses on the left. The building on the right was the Seven Stars Common Lodging House, which was run from the early 1900s by Mr and Mrs Leonard Smith. Past the lodging house were some stone-built cottages, known as the Ox Houses. This whole area is now the site of the police station and garden.

Right: Miss Georgina Jenkinson, Thornbury Guide Captain in the 1930s, was the daughter of 12th Baronet of Eastwood Park, Falfield, George Banks Jenkinson. Following his death in 1915 his widow, Madeline, lived at Clouds, also known as Stokesfield House, now the site of South Gloucestershire Council Offices.

Below: First Thornbury Brownie Pack, with Brown Owl Miss Gale in 1946, at the top of the Mundy Playing Fields. The owl on the toadstool at the front was the totem that the girls danced around and the emblems were imp, nymph, sprite, gnome and fairy. From left to right, back row: Elizabeth Pearce, -?-, -?-, Valerie Birch, Fay Denton, Yvonne Poole. Middle row: Marion Ashcroft, Alicia Rawstorne, Josephine Bull, Miss Gale, Rosemary Alchurch, Barbara Williams, -?-. Front row: Angela Fudge, Janet Flight, Diana Flight, Audrey Pritchard, Barbara Harris, Ann ?, Sheila Smith.

Opposite below: Driver, Victor Worsley in Thornbury Rural District Council's steam wagon, with driver's mate Charles Carter (standing) shortly before the Second World War. The RDC yard was situated near the railway station on the left going towards what is now the junction of Rock Street and Midland Way. The writing near the lamp reveals that this Foden Steam Wagon had a top speed of twelve miles per hour.

Thornbury AFC were runners up in Division IV Bristol and District League seasons 1928/29 and 1929/30. Some of the players were from Oldbury-on-Severn. The matches were played at various sites including Trayhurn's field off Gloucester Road and a field off Eastbury Road. From left to right, back row: -?-, Charlie Pitcher, F. Biddle, ? Wilson, Fred Harris, Jack Oates (goalkeeper), -?-, Victor Knapp, Frank Malpass, Charlie Bennett, -?-. Kneeling: Ron Wall, Arthur Knapp, Ron Tucker, Jim Jones, -?-. Front row, sitting: -?-, Tom Cornock, Jack Thompson, William Knapp, -?-.

Thornbury AFC, *c.* 1949. The club had this motto printed on its fixture cards for many years: 'When the last Great Scorer comes to write against your name, He writes not how you won or lost but how you played the game'. From left to right, standing: John Lewis, George Skuse, Bill Taylor, Des Landsdown, Frank Driscoll, Percy Messenger. Kneeling: Bill Appleby, Ray Rosser, Doug Brealey, Johnny Johnson, Robin Maddison. Terry Williams (with the ball).

Thornbury AFC Second XI, on a wet day in the late 1950s. From left to right, back row: Harold King (Trainer), Roger Longden, Albert Screen, Cyril Lambert, Jack Roberts, Arthur Neale, Alan Bryant, Norman Walker (Secretary). Front row: David Walker, Charlie Fowler, John Whitehead, Godfrey Walker, Roy 'Mackie' Vizard.

Thornbury AFC, Champions of the Bristol Premier Combination (Division Two) in 1966, in front of the pavilion on the Mundy playing fields. From left to right, back row: Roy Wood (Secretary), Rob Ford, Clive Mealing, Alan Wood, Peter Tyrell, Adrian Green, Roger Davis, Mervyn Lacey, Arnold Clark, John Bell (Chairman), Harold King (Trainer). Front row: Ray Shergold, Alan Stone, Graham Smith, Bill Whittaker, Bob Wesley, Brian Harley, John Alker. The caretakers, Mr and Mrs Charlie Roberts, can just be seen at the upstairs window.

Thornbury Youth Club football team won the South Gloucestershire League, 'The Gazette Trophy', in the 1947/48 season. From left to right, back row: Derrick Pearce, Herbert Livall, Fred Kingscott, Colin Rugman. Middle row: Douglas Kingscott, Ray Garland, Desmond Vizard, Ron Taylor. Front row: Ken Roberts, Bob Parker, Herbert Reeves, Ken Worsley, Roy Vizard.

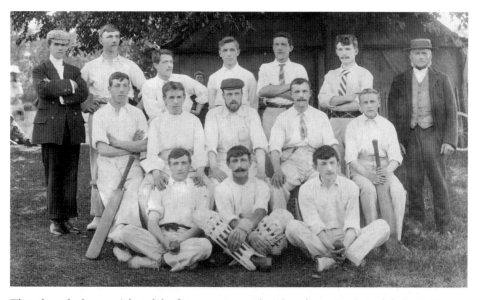

Thornbury had two cricket clubs for many years. The Thornbury Cricket Club, led by Dr E.M. Grace, played matches at the Ship Inn, Alveston, and the Castle Club, led by E Stafford Howard, played its matches on grounds near the castle. This is probably the Castle team in the early 1900s. Around 1919 the teams amalgamated, adopting the emblem of the Stafford knot of Thornbury Castle.

The Thornbury Cricket Club team that played a strong MCC XI, outside the Ship Inn in August 1936. Dr Ted Grace, the son of Dr Edgar Grace, was killed in 1944 while serving with the RAMC in Italy. From left to right, back: Dr Ted Grace. Middle row: Harry Collins, Frank Pullin, Jack Tilley, George Ord, Frank Greenslade, S.J.V. Rouch, Dr D. Prowse. Front row: A.R. Potter, Gilbert Pullin, Dr Edgar M. Grace, Jack Hodges, Jack Thompson.

Dr Edgar Mervyn Grace (left) receiving a watch from Jack Thompson on behalf of the cricket club in December 1948. Dr Grace was captain of the Thornbury Cricket Club for many years; when he retired from play in 1955 he had completed sixty-two years as a playing member. He died in 1974.

Kyneton House, Kington, *c.* 1906. This was the home of the Maclaine family for many years. During the Second World War it was the headquarters of the 6th Maritime Regiment of the Royal Artillery, and from 1960 to 2001 Westwing School occupied the building. It has recently been redeveloped as luxury housing.

A football team made up from staff employed at Kyneton House in 1910.

Kyneton Green Farm, Kington, sketched by Miss Mary Bruton of Oldbury-on-Severn in 1957. Miss Bruton was a frequent visitor to the family of her aunt Ann Knapp (*née* Bruton) who lived at the farm.

Samuel and Sarah Ball and their twins, John and Elsie, born in 1897, at Mill House, Kington, *c.* 1900. John, a private in the Gloucester Regiment, was killed in action in France on 2 September 1916 aged just nineteen. Elsie became a teacher at the Council School, marrying Frederick George Ford, publican of the Barrel Inn in Thornbury. The house still stands but has been extended and modernised.

Above: Jim Davis standing at the gate of Cannon House at the corner of Knapp Road and Hackett Lane. It was so called because of the two small guns that stood in front of the downstairs windows, although it has always been known locally as the Pretty House. The house was built by the Davis brothers who were all in the building trade. Jim Davis died in 1966.

The Anchor Inn at Morton, *c.* 1969. The house to the right in the photograph was known as Morton Villa. There had been a smithy on that site since before 1832, run by Thomas Clark and then by his son, also Thomas Clark. Thomas Clark Jnr's tenth child, Mary, married Charles W. Riddiford and they lived in the house. The buildings were demolished in 1970 to make way for the houses of Charles Close.

Above: Morton Baptist chapel opened in 1834. A Sunday school group, seen here around 1940, are, from left to right, back row: Walter Riddiford, Bob Jefferies, Mrs Winnie Pearce (teacher), David Riddiford, Mr Jim T. Nichols (teacher), Donald Sprackman, Hilda Clarke, Patsy Pearce, Sheila Hewish. Middle row: Miss Mary Nichols (teacher). Joan Riddiford, Marjorie Driver, Jill Sellars, Audrey Pearce, Maureen Sellars, Kathleen Pearce, Clifford Mills, David Sprackman, John Clarke, Joyce Sprackman. Front row: Leslie Gulwell, Michael Hewish, Margaret Howse, Gwyneth Rugman, Beryl Pearce, Jimmy Nichols, Hazel Gray, Rodney Gabb, Diana Matthews, Angela Howell.

Opposite below: Harold James Tapscott with his wife Mary Elizabeth (*née* Trayhurn) outside their grocery store in Clay Lane close to the junction with Crossways Lane, *c.* 1909. This was the birthplace of their son, Norman, before the family emigrated to Canada. The house is now almost unrecognisable due to extensive modernisation, but the gate is unchanged and still in use.

Thomas Ball with his children in front of their well-built corn ricks at Oak Farm, Morton, in 1919. Great care was taken in building these so that the corn-laden heads of the harvested wheat were protected until the threshing engine came round. When the ricks were disturbed many mice and rats ran out. The children are, from left to right: Vera, Clifford, Doris and Harold.

Morton Grange, c. 1931. This is one of the oldest houses in Thornbury, having fifteenth-century origins. It was altered by the Patch family in 1594 with the addition of an upper floor, and has an unusual octagonal crenellated turret projecting on the west side of the house, containing the staircase. The Gingell and Vawdry families lived here in the 1800s.

The Jenkins family playing croquet at Hackett Farm, *c.* 1907. From left to right: Mary Jenkins, Mr William Jenkins, Mrs Ann Jenkins (*née* Ford), Annie Jenkins, William Jenkins Jnr, Albert Jenkins.

The wedding of Maude Burchell and Stanley Kenelm G. Chambers took place on 23 June 1909. The Burchell family lived at the top of Clay Lane near the church; the bride taught at the Church of England School. From left to right, back row: Alfred Burchell, Miss Chambers, Miss Chambers, H.B. Hodgson vicar of Berwick-on-Tweed formerly at Thornbury. Middle row: Miss Chambers, Mrs Alfred Burchell, Annie Burchell, Frank Pinnell, Mrs Katherine Pinnell (*née* Burchell), Dora Burchell, Eleanor Burchell, -?-. Front row: Carpenter John Burchell with Margaret Pinnell, Stanley K.G. Chambers, Maude Burchell, Mrs Annie Burchell with baby Frank Pinnell, Percy Burchill.

Mrs Eliza Jane Riddiford, with her son Levi Screen, at Milbury Heath in the late 1920s. The lean-to washhouse was converted into an annexe shortly after 1946; this later served as the post office for Milbury Heath and Buckover, run by Violet and Fred Riddiford from 1956 to 1989. Mrs Bevan had previously operated Buckover post office from a cottage on the A38.

Situated near Hackett Farm, Buckover National School (Hackett School) opened on 14 February 1876, allowing local children to avoid the long walk into Thornbury; it closed in January 1931. Seen here sometime around 1927 are, from left to right, back row: Kenneth Whitehead, Violet Clutterbuck, Enid Watkins, Grace Curtis, Joyce Peters, Kathleen Lowe, Ken Philips. Middle row: Nellie Exell, Mary Shipp, Joyce Shipp, Nora Watkins, Mary Brace, Stella Shipp, Joyce Clark. Front row: Ernest Brock, Raymond Clark, Reg Payne, George Whitehead, Donald Brace.

two

The Villages

The thirteenth-century tower of St Mary's church, Almondsbury, with its lead-covered spire is a prominent landmark in the Severn Vale, and in the early days of motoring people drove out of Bristol to Almondsbury Hill to see this view of the village with the river and Welsh hills in the distance. Note the number of elm trees; these disappeared when Dutch Elm disease spread rapidly across Britain in the 1960s and '70s.

The junction of Over Lane and Sundays Hill in 1905. A memorial in the form of a stone crucifix was erected here after the First World War; the cross and the land which it stood on were donated by the family of Lt-Col. Richard Chester-Master DSO and Bar who died in Belgium on 30 August 1917.

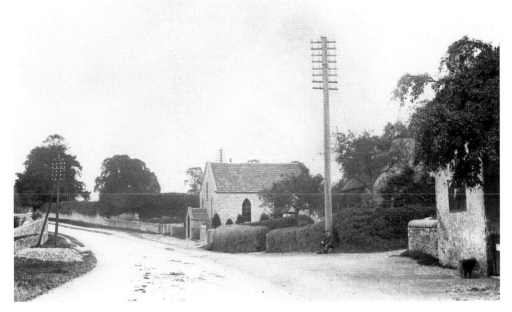

The Wesleyan Methodist Ebenezer chapel at Rudgeway was built in 1890 as a replacement for a nearby smaller chapel. The last service was held at the end of August 2001 following the death, aged ninety-seven, of former chapel steward Mrs Eva Reeves who had fought for several years to keep it open. The building has been converted into a private house. Motorists today would be pleased to see the road as quiet as this scene in the early 1900s.

An etching of Oakleaze, *c.* 1888. This dwelling and its stables were located on Washingpool Hill, primarily to house the horses required to pull the mail coaches up the steep hill on their way from Ireland and South Wales via Aust to London. The expansion of the railway network led to the demise of the horse-drawn Royal Mail coach in the 1840s.

The Grove at Alveston, *c.* 1913. The Bush family inherited the estate in the mid-1800s; it had previously belonged to the Whittington family that included the famous Dick Whittington who became Mayor of London. Edward and his brother, Thomas Bush, were engineers who built engines for some of Brunel's ships and for local coalmines. Later the house was the home of Charles Hill, the Bristol ship builder.

The Bush family, domestic servants and estate workers outside Grove House, *c.* 1900. From left to right, front row: maid Jane Davis, who later married Charles Weeks (second from right in the back row), -?-, Miss Clementina Bush, Edward Bush (1820-1908), Mrs (Emily) William Brice Salmon (*née* Bush). The Jamaican woman behind Emily Salmon is Elizabeth Snipe (known in Alveston as Granny Snipe); her grave records that she was born in Jamaica in 1841, died at the Grove 11 May 1905 and was 'for 43 years a faithful servant to Mrs W.B. Salmon'.

Above: Charles Hill at Grove House in 1969. The Bristol Marina was once Albion Yard, site of the shipyard of Charles Hill & Sons Ltd. *Miranda Guinness*, the last ship to be launched in Bristol, was constructed there in 1976 after which the yard closed following 156 years of shipbuilding.

Right: William Stacey, butler to Charles Hill, in the gardens of Grove House. Born in 1890, William Stacey worked as a youngster at Thornbury Castle in the position of footman to E. Stafford Howard. He returned to the area to work for Charles Hill from 1955 to 1969.

The Stutchbury family at the rear of The Firs, their home in Alveston, *c.* 1905. Samuel Stutchbury was once a consulting mining engineer; his wife, Maria, was the daughter of Thornbury solicitor Richard Scarlett. Their three daughters were called Sarah Mary, Elsie Gertrude and Helen Maud. Samuel's sister, Annie White Stutchbury, was the first wife of Thornbury doctor Edward Mills Grace.

The Collins family of Greenhill Villa, The Square, Alveston, in the 1920s. Thomas Collins was the foreman at Greenhill Quarry; he married Alice Louisa Pickthorne in 1900. With the exception of Jim, all the sons worked at the quarry until it closed in the 1930s, when they went to work for the Bristol Aeroplane Co. Ltd. From left to right, back row: Martin, Gladys, Arthur and Elsie. Front row: Jack, Thomas Collins, Reg, Alice Collins with baby Jim and Gilbert.

The first crossing of the *May Queen* on 1 August 1926. This was the first passenger launch used when Newport architect Enoch Williams revived the Aust to Beachley ferry route with the starting of the Old Passage Ferry Co. Carts and cars were winched into the boat. *Princess Ida*, a wooden car ferry, replaced it in 1931.

The *Severn Princess* with the Severn Bridge being constucted in the background, *c.* 1964. As demand grew for the ferry service, the steel vessels *Severn Queen* and *Severn King* were introduced in around 1935, followed in 1959 by a larger ship, the *Severn Princess*. The three vessels offered crossings every twenty-five minutes, finally carrying 25,000 cars a month. Despite the dangerous tides, shifting sandbanks and often dreadful weather conditions, no passengers were ever killed or seriously injured on these ferries.

Tea rooms could be found along many of the routes used by motorists travelling to and from the ferry at Aust. The Cliff House Tea Gardens were advertised in the *Severn-side Magazine* of August 1925 as 'an ideal spot for a quiet holiday overlooking Severn & Welsh Hills. Bus 5 mins. Own farm produce. Terms moderate. Tennis. Large & small parties catered for. Apply Mrs G. Watkins'.

The rear of the house known as Esperanza, Aust, in 1938. There is some evidence to suggest that this may have had its origins as a longhouse of the type once common in farming communities in south west England and Wales. The humans lived in one end with the animals at the other end; by the sixteenth century a passage separated the dwelling house from the byre.

The tangled wreckage of the Leeds to Bristol night mail train, which collided in fog with a goods train near the road bridge over the railway line at Charfield in the early hours of Saturday 13 October 1928. The collision ignited gas cylinders which were still being used in older stock to supply gas lighting in the carriages and the resulting fire added to the devastation caused by the impact.

Grave of Victims of Railway Disaster at Charfield, Oct.13th, 1928. Charfield Old Church.

The London, Midland & Scottish Railway Co. erected a memorial on the communal grave situated at the old church of St James at Churchend, Charfield. As the fire had been so severe it was difficult to ascertain how many of the passengers on the mail train had been killed, and there has always been some mystery attached to the possibility that two children were killed, although no one ever reported them missing.

Charfield Congregational chapel, *c.* 1920. The sum of £290 required for the building was raised by public subscription while the land and stone were granted by Lord Ducie. The chapel opened on 23 October 1851 and is still in use today as the United Reform church, but the ornate gas lamps have gone.

Charfield Mills were built on an earlier mill site by Samuel and William Long in the early 1800s. For many years a fabric called 'doeskin' was manufactured but at the beginning of the 1890s the mills were sold to Tubbs Lewis. This company manufactured such items as bobbins, crochet hooks and display racks and cards to support the making of elastic and ribbons at its main mills at Kingswood. A variety of other small businesses also operated from the Charfield Mills.

Workers at Charfield Mills *c.* 1910, including James Lucas, who later became a blacksmith in the village (second from left, back row). The Mills became known locally as the Pin Mills after the arrival of a pinmaking firm, Perkins and Marmont, early in the twentieth century.

Wotton Road, Charfield, *c.* 1910. On the right is the shop belonging to tailor and draper Mr G. Richards who was also running a post office. Next to it is the business of James Lucas; 'Shoeing & General Smith'. The building is now occupied by coal merchants Jones Brothers.

A girl, probably posing for the camera, stands outside the Red Lion Inn in Cromhall in the early 1900s; with her yoke and buckets she may have been milking the cows or fetching water from the well. Road widening caused the large tree at Long Cross, believed to be an elm, to be removed in the 1950s.

Men outside the Red Lion Inn, Cromhall, in August 1901. From left to right, standing: landlord Ted Collins, Gilbert Cole, Percy Pick, George 'Kipper' Fisher. Sitting: Bill 'Tittler' Pick, Frank 'Bumper' Bell. The building is now a private house.

William Arthur and Dora King with their children; Edgar, Hartley, Wilfred and baby Frederick, at Old Green Farm, Earthcott, *c.* 1912. Parts of the roof date back to before 1600 and old ships' timbers were used in the structure of the house. The Kings came from Somerset in the early 1900s and purchased the farm from the Bush estate in 1937.

Hartley (left) and Edgar King at Old Green Farm, Earthcott, *c.* 1920. The Bamford stationary engine enabled farmers to power all sorts of machinery.

Above: The forge at Elberton, *c.* 1907. Blacksmith Thomas Robbins is on the far left with his daughters, Annie and Carrie, on the right.

Left: Blacksmith Jack Hammond (right) purchased the forge at Elberton in the late 1940s. In the early 1950s he added a garage workshop. The shoeing of working horses was in decline but there was a growing demand for wrought-iron gates.

Above: Eastwood Park, Falfield, *c.* 1930. Charles Jenkinson, First Earl of Liverpool, bought the estate in the eighteenth century and Sir George Jenkinson built this house in 1865. By 1935 the Home Office owned the property and in wartime used it as 'The Ministry of Home Security Air Raid Precautions School'; Civil Defence courses continued there until 1968. Acquired by the DHHS in 1969 it provided a Course Centre for engineering staff in the NHS. Today the house is a Training and Conference Centre.

Right: Nellie Hughes standing outside Eastwood Lodge, *c.* 1914. Nellie, whose father, William Hughes, worked on the estate, used to wait for carriages coming from the Park; she would open the gates and be given a few coppers in return.

Thornbury photographer Alexander Sutherland took this picture of the 69ft whale that beached at Littleton-on-Severn on 5 January 1885. George Sindry brought his two steam traction engines from Olveston and, with the help of huge chains, the whale had been hauled further inshore. Overnight Littleton became famous; the Midland Railway put on special trains to Thornbury to cater for thousands of visitors. The carcass was eventually taken to Bristol to be cut down for manure.

Enoch Durnell was foreman at the brickworks at Littleton-on-Severn. His wife, Bella, was the first person to see the whale. From left to right, back row: Walter Durnell, Lucy Durnell (daughter of Moses White), -?-, Isabella Durnell (*née* White), and Enoch Durnell, some time in the 1920s.

Right: Launched in 1830 at Bridgwater, the *Matilda* was a sloop, the most common form of sailing vessel around the coastline. These little vessels carried farm produce, coal, sand and so on; bricks manufactured at riverside clay pits were taken to the towns down and across the estuary. The *Matilda* was operated out of Littleton for many years by Moses and James White.

Below: Reflections in the water on a calm day at Oldbury Pill. At low tide the pill had very little water in it, but plenty of mud, once described by Miss Mary Bruton as 'the softest, smoothest, most affectionate mud you ever saw – if you encounter it you will surely take it home with you; boys and ducks love it but it has been the despair of generations of mothers!'

Oldbury-on-Severn AFC in 1910. From left to right, back row: George Russell, Albert Highnam, Stan Perry, Bert Williams, Fred Andrews, Gilbert Millard, -?-, John Aspland. Front row: Tommy Vizzard, ? Williams, ? Bennett, Arthur Thomas, Jess Davies, Harry Williams, George Jones.

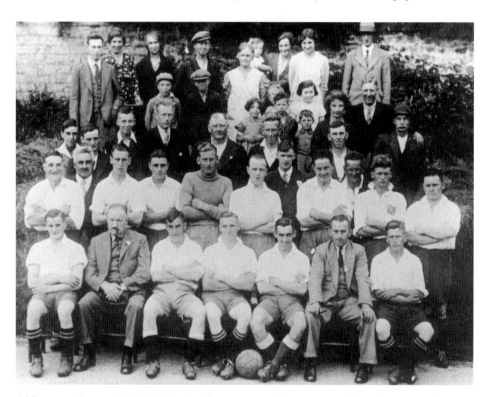

Oldbury-on-Severn AFC in 1935/36. The team members are named here but most of the supporters are also known. From left to right, back row: Cyril Hopkins, Ernest Osbourne, Leslie Ford, Joe Rugman, George Walker, Ronald Davis, Harry Till, Tom Cornock. Front row: Wilfred Morgan, Alfred Laver (President), Wilbur Knapp, Ernest Hopkins, Robert Curtis, Arthur Knapp (Chairman), Victor Jones.

The wedding of builder Robert Parker Curtis and Grace Ellen Shipp took place at Oldbury church in August 1939. From left to right, back row: Marie Shipp, Victor Jones, Robert Curtis, Grace Shipp, Herbert J. Shipp, Joan Burchell. Front: Josephine Jones, the groom's niece.

Oldbury-on-Severn Brownies, on the Pound, c. 1944. Some of the girls were wartime evacuees. From left to right, back row: Rita Rugman, Marian Davis, Marion Fall, Joan Seaman, Ann Gazzard (Brown Owl), Jill Loftus, Audrey Fall, Valerie Ford. Front row: Mary Ford, Betty Knapp, Rosemary Griffiths, Shirley Savery, Audrey Rugman, Brenda Keedwell, Sheila Clutterbuck.

Above: Children enjoying themselves in the school playground in Oldbury-on-Severn in the early 1960s. The bell was removed not long after this photograph was taken as it had become unsafe.

Opposite above: The fire brigade was in attendance at Oldbury parish church for the wedding of Phyllis Clark and Thornbury fireman Jack Clutterbuck in September 1932. Jack ran the Paragon Motor Works in St Mary Street. The fireman in the cap to the right of the bride is Mr A.H. Wilkins, draper of Manchester House, Thornbury. To his right are Mrs Keedwell and, without a hat, Mrs Arthur (Maisie) Knapp.

Opposite below: The Oldbury Black Gang would turn up at local weddings whether invited or not! Helping to celebrate the wedding of Robert Nelmes and Phyllis Gazzard in the early 1930s were, from left to right: Jim Allen, Gilbert 'Nobby' Brown, Fred Griffiths, Lewis Hall with policeman's helmet, -?-.

Left: Mary Bruton, aged twenty. Born in Oldbury-on-Severn in September 1890, daughter of wheelwright/builder Charles Bruton and Annis (*née* Rugman), Miss Bruton lived in the village until her death in 1984. She was a well-known character and was very involved in village life. She was artistic, musical and had a great interest in preserving the history of the area.

Below: Miss Mary Bruton at Ullswater in the Lake District on 10 July 1955, presenting the helmet on which she had painted her own design of a bluebird at the request of Lady Campbell. The recipient was water speed record breaker Donald Campbell, who was killed on Coniston Water on 4 January 1967 in his boat, *Bluebird K7*.

Opposite above: Cidermaking in the early 1900s at Bennett's licensed farmhouse in Cowhill, known as the Star Inn. The area around Oldbury-on-Severn was renowned for its cider made from apples grown in local orchards. Originally the apples were crushed in stone mills powered by horses but later a steam engine, taken from farm to farm, would work the mills. On the far left, at the back, is Joe Bennett with William Knapp on the far left, front.

A picnic on the Severn Bank in the 1920s. From left to right: Jim Creed, Sally Creed, Joan Smart, Ada Smart. Sally and Ada were daughters of Oldbury–on–Severn farmer and carrier Walter Riddle. Jim Creed was originally from Tytherington but the family lived at Malvern. Ada's husband, Fred Smart, was a butcher in Gloucester. Joan Smart died of meningitis as a teenager.

Joe Cornock and his son Hector removing salmon from kypes at low tide at Horse Pool, just off Shipperdine near Oldbury-on-Severn, c. 1912. The Severn Estuary was well known for its old tradition of fishing for salmon, flat fish, eels, elvers and shrimps.

Salmon putchers were put to a different use at the wedding of Nora Knapp and fisherman Tony Banfield at Oldbury-on-Severn church in 1965. The adults are, from left to right: Nat Jenner with putcher, best man Ken James, Jackie Raymond, Tony Banfield, Nora Knapp, Ashley Ford with putcher, Tony Meredith with putcher. The bridesmaids were Wendy Knapp, Peggy Cullimore, Julie Cullimore and Carol Knapp. The sign hanging from the putchers reads 'Tony's Best Catch'.

A view from Eastcombe Hill overlooking Haw Lane towards the village of Olveston, *c.* 1927. The buildings, from left to right, are: Eastcombe House, the doctor's surgery built as a Free Methodist chapel in 1861, Haw Leaze and The Nurseries, which has been renamed Hawthornes.

Members of the Queen Victoria Diamond Jubilee Celebration Committee gathered in front of a huge bonfire stack at The Park, Old Down, in 1897. From left to right, back row: -?-, W. Harford, William Haskins, W.A. Ward, George Pullin, Col. Salmon, R. Todd, J. King, A. Pitcher. Second row: J. Stephens, ? Alpass, F.W. Ward, Fred Olive, H. Wintle, George Stephens, Roy Pitcher (infant). Front: -?-, H. Humphries.

Above: Olveston Scouts on a camping trip to West Bay, Dorset, c. 1929. From left to right, back row: –?–, Mr David Kee (Scoutmaster), William Frost, Eric Pope, Joseph Caswell. Front row: Stanley Lansdown, Frank Edwards, Ernest Grosvenor, Peter Groves, Edward Greves, –?–, Ralph Frost.

Above: Children at Olveston and Elberton School in 1913. From left to right, back row: Elsie Cullimore, Win Pane, Bill Cole, Win Neale, Beatrice Davis, -?-, headmaster William Green. Middle row: -?-, Edith Lansdown, Maud Gregory, Ida Skuse, Doris White, -?-, -?-, Kath Saxton, Eddie Leakey. Front row: Frank Lansdown, Bert Downs (who died in March 2005 aged 104), Edward Haskins, William Davis, Arthur Stephens, Archie Pick.

Right: Mr William Green, headmaster of Olveston and Elberton School from October 1884 to January 1916, with other members of staff.

Opposite below: Ninety-nine children pose in Olveston and Elberton National School's celebration photograph to mark the building of a second extension to the school in 1871. The previous 1854 extension is on the right. At that time, the staff consisted of the headmaster and mistress William and Emma Wilkes with pupil teachers William Green and Henry Oakhill. The vicar is either Revd Canon Moseley or Revd A.G. Stallard.

Left: Mr Lionel Edmonds, headmaster of Olveston and Elberton School from 1916 to 1934, with Lucy Durnell (sitting on his right) and other members of staff.

Below: Children at Olveston and Elberton National School in 1929. From left to right, back row: Freda Saxton, Elsie Young, Vera Dyer, Jessie Biddle, Violet Dyer, Minnie Selman, Win Parsons. Second row: Jack Edmonds, Maurice Stinchcombe, Ernest Grosvenor, Fred Spencer, Fred Grove, Ronald Frost, Frank Curtis. Third row: Betty Woodrow, Irene Garner, Gladys Hemsell, Elsie Dyer, Madeline Bacon, Betty Judge, Vera Jenkins. Front row: Molly Cole, Marjorie Haskins, Lionel Edmonds (headmaster), Olive Teague, Helen Taylor.

Children at Olveston and Elberton School in 1953. From left to right, back row: Chris Browning, Kelson Ball, Terry Blacker, Barry Curtis, Alan Grove, Michael Brown, Michael Winder. Middle row: Headmistress Mrs Macdonald, Cynthia Tudor, Diana Adams, Caroline Frost, Rosalind Trott. Front row: Derek Edwards, Gillian Northover, Hazel Jeffries, Julie Latty, Jennifer Wigmore, Cynthia Teague, Mary Northover, John Hatton.

Mrs Macdonald was headmistress of Olveston and Elberton School from April 1953 to April 1966, having previously been a teacher at the Council School in Thornbury. From left to right: Mrs Mary Hallett, vicar of Olveston Revd David Cartwright, Mrs Doris Macdonald (*née* Hendy), Miss Win Jefferies.

Left: Olveston post office at the junction of The Street and Vicarage Lane. Built in the 1840s, the building was a shop and post office in Victorian times. For a while it was a china store, then a boot and shoe shop before finally reverting to a post office again in 1936. It ceased trading in 2002 and is now a private house.

Below: A rare photograph taken around 1951 at Church Hill, Olveston, showing one of the lorries run by Till's Transport of Thornbury. The driver, Jack Miles, lived at Church Hill; he had formerly driven Sentinel steam wagons at Harn Hill Quarry.

Opposite below: Mr Lewis' class at Pilning School, *c.* 1959. From left to right, back row: Klaus Dieter (German visitor), Stephen Blake, David Boucher, Andrew Cotter, -?-, -?-, Ronald Pritchard, Kevin Thompson, Stephen Parfitt. Second row: Andre Butt, Kevin Lewis, Leslie Jones, Veronica Mills, Carolyn Barlow, Sylvia Coombs, -?-, -?-, -?-, -?-. Third row: -?-, Linda Hall, Suzanne Hooper, Valerie Stedman, Elizabeth Stirk, Helen Hopkins (cousin of the German boy), Irene Taylor, Susan Heyward, Janice Osmond, Rowena Thomas, Josephine Day. Front row: William Relton, Nicholas Tyson, -?-, Michael Stokes, -?-, Geoffrey White, Robert Weeks.

Above: Children at Pilning School in the early 1890s, when the headmistress was Miss Stock. The boy sixth from left in the second row from the back is believed to be George Edward Howse, who later went on to marry Mabel Ann Sims, also of Pilning.

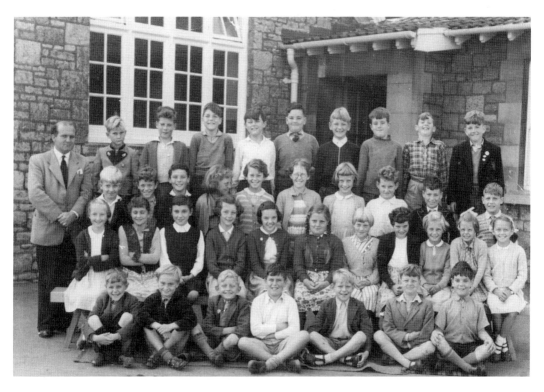

Above: Miss Branun's class at Pilning School, *c.* 1959. From left to right, back row: Richard Plumley, Jeffery White, John White, Alan Coleman, Ted Parrott, Ivor Oxan, Phillip Plant, Peter Ball, Eddie Butt. Second row: Lyn White, Roy Constable, Vivian Poole, Melanie Hallum, –?–, Lynne Beardsmore, –?–, Wendy Poole, Jeffery Hardacre, Tony Stutter. Third row: Louise Easter, –?–, –?–, Jennifer Meachen, Linda Burke, Lynne Braznell, Madeline Priest, Hazel Shoemark, Annette Twynham, Linda Long, Linda Ball. Front row: Anthony Stedman, Brian Heyward, Vernon Mills, Kevin Thomas, –?–, John Barton, John Lasek, Michael Edwards.

Children at Redwick and Northwick School in 1949. From left to right, back row: Jean ?, -?-, Grace Stevens, Sandra ?, -?-, John Bishop, John Lampard, Edward Spratt, Michael Cox, Michael Say, Teacher Josephine Paul. Front row: -?-, -?-, Gillian Stevens, Barbara Cox, -?-, Mary Drew, -?-, -?-, Elizabeth Watkins, -?-, Ken Barry (who later kept Aust post office).

Above: A baby clinic in the early 1950s, possibly held in Severn Beach Methodist Hall. On the extreme left is Mrs Stride, and Nurse Mason is weighing the baby.

Opposite below: Children with their teacher, Miss Clements, at Redwick and Northwick School in 1901. Jim Paul, aged six, is third from the left in the front row. He was the son of carter Alfred Paul and his wife Mary (*née* Parker).

Girls with tambourines at Rockhampton School, *c.* 1925. Judging from the expressions on their faces, posing for the camera was a serious business! From left to right, back row: Grace Shipp, Gertie Shipp, Freda Shipp, Eva Grove (?). Front row: Marie Shipp, Phyllis Child.

Above: It is believed that this study of a child at school sometime in 1906 may have been taken at Rockhampton School. The boy is William Charles Elias Peters who was born on 26 November 1897 at Duckhole, the son of Charles Peters and Caroline (*née* Mills) who lived at Chapel Farm, Lower Morton, in the early 1900s. Later, Charles Peters became the bailiff at Vilner Farm, Thornbury, which was owned by Mrs Violet Mundy. William followed in his father's footsteps to become bailiff at the same farm; he died in 1957.

Opposite below: Reg (left) and Fred Riddiford, sons of Tom and Kate Riddiford, with their twenty-seater coach in 1948. The business was based at Coopers Farm, Newton (now part of Rockhampton); the coaches were well known in the Thornbury area, taking children to and from school and being hired for all sorts of outings.

Above: Living at Rockhampton, but probably married at Hill church in 1926, were Margaret Pinnell and O'Decimus Shipp. Most of the Shipp family moved to Oldbury Naite in 1927. From left to right, back row: Frank Pinnell, John Shipp, Elsie Shipp, Hannah Shipp, Les Shipp, Herbert Shipp, Bob Mills, Katherine Shipp, baby Herbert Shipp, Nellie Thorne. Middle row: Donald Shipp, Ivy Shipp, Ivor Shipp, O'Decimus Shipp, Margaret Pinnell, Annie Burchell, Richard Shipp. Front row: Gertie Shipp, Marie Shipp, Grace Shipp.

A group of children on Tockington Green assist the photographer while two mothers observe from their houses in the background, *c.* 1917. The building with the porch was a post office and is now a private house.

Parishioners gathered on the Green at Tockington to celebrate the coronation of King George VI in 1937 prior to a fancy dress procession to The Park at Old Down, headed by the Easter Compton Brass Band.

Alfred Jarrett (centre left) holding a handful of hay for the horse, *c.* 1900. He operated as a wheelwright and carpenter from his yard at The Limes until his death in 1914. His senior workman, Walter Durnell, then took on the business but it ceased with his retirement in the late 1940s.

An etching of Tockington House (later known as Tockington Manor) from a sale brochure in 1888 when the house, together with 1,200 acres of land, was sold on the winding up of the Peach estate. The house was the headquarters of the Tockington Militia Regiment throughout the Napoleonic War, and was later used during the Second World War as the Engineering Project Design Department of the Bristol Aeroplane Co., before being converted into a private school for boys in 1947.

Tortworth Court was built in the gothic style in the early 1850s for the Second Earl of Ducie by architect Samuel Sanders Teulon, who, in 1866, designed the Tyndale Monument above North Nibley, visible from the Tortworth Estate. The house, owned by the prison department until 1987, is now a hotel. Teulon also designed the terraced gardens.

Men clearing the remains of a large tree on Tortworth Green stop work to pose for the camera, *c.* 1907. The building in the background was an orphanage founded by Countess Julia, wife of the Third Earl Ducie; it closed in the early 1900s and is now a private house.

Right: One of the Tortworth estate houses near to the church was the home of the Keynton family, *c.* 1910. From left to right: Victoria, William, Harold, Albert Keynton (plumber and carpenter), Jane Keynton (*née* Roberts), Hilda. William became a butler at Tortworth Court. Victoria (Queenie) lived in Bristol and died in 2002 aged 101. Hilda married Arthur Boyt of Porch House, Tytherington.

Below: A group in the early 1900s outside Tytherington post office and grocers, run by Florence and Frederick Churchill Humphries. Mr Humphries, known as Putty to the villagers as he was also a glazier, decorator and plumber, is on horseback. The old village pound was demolished when the building, known as Liberty House, was erected in 1900.

George Boyt Jnr sitting outside Porch House, *c.* 1929. The Harwoods, who were local bankers, probably built the house, formerly known as Bromwich's, around 1660. From 1851 it was home to three generations of the Boyt family. George Boyt was a pork butcher; his son George and then grandson Arthur continued the business until 1964.

The Tytherington Section, 40 Platoon D Company 6th Battalion Gloucester Regiment of the Home Guard in the 1940s. From left to right, back row: Bill Nelmes, Lionel Livall, Bill Lewis, George Jobbins, John Millard. Second row: Glyn Goulden, Charlie Poole, Eric Pitt, Bob Williams, Dennis Ponting, Eric Bryant, Roy 'Tojo' Livall. Third row: Harold Pedrick, Jack Monks, Tom Woodward, Bert Nelmes, Norman Curtis, Dick Pope, Bertie Livall, Ted Livall. Front row: Jack Dicker, Harold Nelmes, Arthur Pollard, Mr Reg Alchurch, Mr Jackson, Robin Hanscombe, Ted Smith of Grovesend, Percy Always, Reg Cassell.

Tytherington children at a fancy dress event in the early 1940s, possibly during War Weapons Week, which raised money for the war effort. Winston Churchill's hat declares it has a message from the Prime Minister but sadly the message itself is not legible. From left to right: Dennis Nelmes, Margaret Wilson, Alfred Kingston, Violet Kingston.

Another group from the same event in which most of the village participated. The sign on the right reads 'Blow the Ration'. From left to right: -?-, Mary Cornock, -?-, evacuee Gerald Dicker, Doris Smith, -?-, Grace Smith, Joyce Monks.

Left: The vicar and other officers of St James's church, *c.* 1947. The first mention of a stone church at Tytherington is from AD 1160. From left to right: Vic Smith, Bob Williams, Canon Arthur John Kitson (vicar of Tytherington 1919 to 1948), Arthur Cassell, Bert Davis, Bill Poole, Reg Cassell.

Below: Part of the celebrations in Tytherington for the coronation of Queen Elizabeth II in 1953. From left to right: -?-, Yvonne Collis, Gillian Cook, Phillip Hall, Dorothy Clutterbuck, Judith Waddleton, Michael Green, -?-, -?-, David Hall, Michael Howell, Mervyn Pitt, -?-, -?-, Colin Ponting. The small girl in front is Marlene Button.

Above: The opening of the new village hall in Tytherington, *c.* 1953. From left to right, front row: Richard Davis, Gordon Payne, Billy Baxter, Michael Davis, Mrs Tom Pitt, Mrs Leakey. Second row: Judith Wadleton, Wendy Ponting, -?-, -?-, ? Shepherd, Mrs Pitt, Mr Livall, Alice Johnson. Third row: Esme Shepherd, -?-, Norah English, Ken Livall, Valerie Pitt, Beryl Pitt, Vera Hetherington, -?-.

Right: Post lady Mrs Annie 'Ciss' Sansum, with St James's church in the background, *c.* 1938. Annie was the daughter of F.C. Humphries and his wife Florence (*née* Tratman); she was the sub-postmistress in Tytherington from 1933 to 1939. The old red telephone box is still in position.

Tytherington AFC, participants in the Wotton–under–Edge League 1900/01. From left to right, back row: Thomas Davis, Lawford Blanchard, Frank Kingscott, Lebby Collins, -?-, Yank Livall, Bill Livall, Austin Livall. Middle row: Truey Smith, ? Long, Pecky Boyt, Bill Cornock, Frank Humphries, Jock Fry, Ted Livall. Front row: Fred Vizard, -?-, ? Arkle, ? Fry, G. Blanchard.

Tytherington AFC Champions Tytherington Rocks/Iron Acton League, 1944. From left to right, back row: Les Taylor, Ernie Lambert, John Lewis, Frank Driscoll, Bert Nelmes, John Sage, Perce Hand, Ambrose Johnson, Ted Pitt, Arthur Boyt. Front row: Cliff Ponting, Reg Vowles, Reg Collins, Wilf Humphries, Gilbert Reeves, Don Vizard.

three

Thornbury Grammar School 1606-2006

The old Grammar School buildings at the bottom of Castle Street were the subject chosen by Miss Mary Bruton to sketch for the 1947 Grammar School Christmas card. Miss Bruton taught art at the school in 1947 and music in 1949.

Mr Charles Hackwell Ross MA (seen here in the centre around 1908) was headmaster of Thornbury Grammar School from 1907 to 1932. With his arrival, a school uniform was adopted and the school obtained permission to use the Attwells arms as a badge. Harold Higgins is in the second row from the back, second from left. The boy standing in the doorway is Dudley Cullimore.

The hockey team in 1912. Girls were admitted to the school in 1906, with Emily Lippiatt (later Mrs Lanham) being the first girl to attend. From left to right, back row: teacher Miss Jenkins, Nora Pearce, Mrs Ross the headmaster's wife. Middle row: Paddy Dean, Clarice Lashford, Elsie Ball, -?-. Front row: Rotha Pearce, Florence Fentiman, Bertha Exell, Cissie Sindry, ? Lee.

The football team, *c.* 1912. Second from left, back row, is the master, Mr W.G. Rabley, who was appointed in 1911, teaching at the school for forty years. He was president of Thornbury Tennis Club, which he captained for twenty-one years, and vice-president of the Cricket Club. He also found time to be a Special Constable, a Parish Councillor and Chairman of the Thornbury Scouts Association. He died in 1956.

Above: The staff of Thornbury Grammar School in 1922. From left to right, back row: Mr W.G. Rabley, Mr B. Stafford Morse, Miss D. Mortimore, Miss D. Ashcroft. Front row: Mr B. Laycock, Mr Charles H. Ross, Miss Griffin.

Below: Thornbury Grammar School girls with headmaster Mr Ross, *c.* 1924. The girls' tunics were dark green and, until 1933, had a white braid trim at the bottom of the skirt.

The Grammar School, Thornbury.

Above: Thornbury Grammar School boys with Mr Ross, *c.* 1924. Mr Ross was said to be a most kindly man and after his death in 1956, old Thornburians remembered him with respect and affection.

Below: A group on the sports field behind the school in 1927. Mons Smith's father was Alfred Smith, Master Baker who worked for Thompson's bakery at the top of the High Street. Bernice Gill's grandfather was Alfred Gill, a Thornbury train driver. Mons Smith and Bernice Gill, both now in their nineties, are still friends! From left to right, back: Mr Ross. Standing: Mons (Mary) Smith, Joyce Bruton, Elizabeth Grace, Doreen Williams, Bernice Gill. Kneeling: Frances Henson, Diana Cotter. Sitting: Molly Cotter.

Pupils in the early 1930s with teacher Miss Thomlinson (who married Roy Luce). From left to right, back row: William Appleby, Norman Taylor, Leslie Ford, -?-, Royce Gazzard, Dick Gray, -?-, Eric Garrett of Park Farm, Tom Daniels, -?-. Middle row: Isobel Jones, Clarice Morgan, Alice Collins, Diane Webb, Marjorie West, Joan Gazzard, Betty Boyt, Ruth Pullin, Brenda Pullin. Front row: Joan Dearing, Freda Ford, Gwen Meredith, Mary Nichols, Edna Bartlett.

R.W. Jackson MA BSc was appointed headmaster in 1932 when the new building was opened. The staff in the centre of this school photograph, taken in October 1934, are, from left to right: Mr Bull, Mr F.H. Pollard (Chemistry and Physics), Mr W.G.. Rabley (Woodwork and Sport), Mr B. Stafford Morse (History, Latin. RE), Senior Master Mr B. Laycock (Maths), headmaster Mr Jackson, Senior Mistress Miss Adrienne Dicker (English), Miss E. Smith (Commercial and French), -?-, Miss B.M. Thomlinson, Miss S. Barlow (Botany/Biology), Miss Tanner.

Miss Barlow's class, *c.* 1933. When Mr Jackson left in 1934 the school houses of Howard (red), Stafford (blue) and Clare (gold) had been established and in December that year the first school magazine, known as The Thornburian, had been issued. From left to right, back row: -?-. Second row: Joan Dearing, Beatty Clifford, Barbara Bruton, -?-, Vera ?, -?-, Alice Walker, Betty Sealey, Phyllis Cottrell, Ethel Weeks. Third row: -?-, Nellie Taylor, Betty Pullin, Vera Hetherington, Margaret Maggs, Betty Boyt, -?-. Front row: ? Watkins, -?-.

A group of dignitaries (probably school governors), *c.* 1937. Mr S.J.V. Rouch BSc became headmaster in 1934 and held the position for twenty-nine years. From left to right, back row: C.P. Taylor, Revd H.E. McLeod, -?-, Revd F E Harker, Dr E.M. Grace. Middle row: -?-, Captain R.A. Bennett JP (Chairman of Governors), Sidney H. Gaynor, -?-, S.J.V. Rouch. Front row: Mrs F.H. Grace, -?-, -?-, Mrs Rouch.

School prefects in the quadrangle in 1940. Many evacuees joined the school and older pupils took on war duties such as fire watching and youth service or joined the ARP, ATC and Home Guard. From left to right, back row: Henry Knight, W. Vizard. Middle row: Nellie Exell, A. Hills, Jane Veale, H. Lee, H. Holpin, Edna Bartlett, Ron Lewis, Enid Watkins. Front row: Barbara Pierce, W. Batten, Mary Turner, Mr Rouch, L. Taylor, Audrey Lydford, J. Hosken.

The cast of *Macbeth* in 1946. From left to right, back row: Phillip Clutterbuck, Micky Teague, Patsy Harvey, John White, David Biggin. Second row: Mary Nicholls, Brian Selwood, Pauline Robson, Mavis Gill, Mac Summers, Paddy Morissey, Roy Barge. Third row: Viking Rex Cooper, Mike Lewis, Eileen Pullin, Peter Winstone, Mary Rouch, Ted Addis, Barbara Neads, Cyril Jeffery, Viking Laurie Hummerstone. Front: Jennifer Rouch, Josephine Paul.

Unfortunately, there are few known class photographs from the 1940s. However, this one shows pupils in 1946. From left to right, back row: Roy Barge, Sally May, Mac Summers, Ruth Shepherd, Alan Hucker, Mavis Gill, Roy Wood, Mary Cornock, Chris Woodward. Second row: Gillian Thiery, Mary Clutterbuck, Paddy Morrisey, Doreen Parker, Beryl Palmer, Hilda Webb, Annette Gazzard, Betty Myring, Jean Rudledge, Pearl Fuller. Third row: Margaret Thorne, Joan Timbrell, Ula Reynolds, John White, ? Jackson, Desmond Cooper, Patsy Harvey, David Biggin, Pat Brown, Barbara Fear, Sylvia Gopsill. Front row: Barbara Penney, Keith Smythe, Dorothy Rudledge.

A snowball fight on the school field, c. 1947.

Above: The first post-war rugby team, *c.* 1947. From left to right, back row: Hugh Thomas, Alan Perry, Cyril Hathway. Middle row: Mike Pierce, Mike Lewis, Ian Harris, Ron Vizard, Windsor Davis, Peter Nott, John King, John Hannaford. Front row: Mr Rouch, Alan Hucker, Dennis Hawkins, Norman Daley Captain, Ray England, Cyril Jeffries, Mr Harwood.

Below: Girls give a dance demonstration on the playing field on Speech Day, *c.* 1948. During the Second World War part of the playing field had to be fenced off as sheep pasture to save petrol in mowing it. One night in 1940 some of the sheep escaped and ate the best Brussels sprouts in the headmaster's garden!

Above: The cricket First XI in 1949. From left to right, back row: Gordon Haines, David Hamilton, Terry Williams. Middle row: Mr Rouch, Donald Biddle, Ron Vizard, Alan Hucker, Mervyn Pierce, Mr Johnson. Front row: Ray Redden, Michael Lewis, John Hannaford, Norman Daley, Derek Hawkins.

Below: The prefects, *c.* 1949. From left to right, back row: Michael Teague, Gerald Dicker, Windsor Davies, Roland Rosser, Stuart Rugman. Middle row: Ula Reynolds, Brian Selwood, Mary Clutterbuck, Joan Timbrell, Brenda Bradford, Michael Lewis, Jean Rudledge. Front row: Anne Pritchard, John Hannaford, Jennifer Rouch, Mr Rouch, Senior Mistress Miss Cook, Peter Hardman, Marian Thomas, Peter Nott.

Left: The impressive athletics display at Sports Day, 1950. The Gymnastic Club used to do extra physical training after school until 6 p.m. every Friday. PE instructor Mr Brian Young assists as Derek Hawkins leaps above one of the Fowell brothers.

Below: Swimming was introduced as a sport in 1935 with lessons at the Bathings; the baths closed in the early 1950s after pupil Peter Hardman became ill possibly as a result from swimming there. The school then held its swimming galas at the Blue Lagoon, Severn Beach. From around 1954 Mr Pedlar taught swimming by taking groups to the Broad Weir Baths on Saturday mornings.

Opposite above: The prefects, *c.* 1950. From left to right, back row: Frances Riddiford, Donald Malpass, Eric Locke, Patricia Brown, David Hamilton, Desmond Cooper, Dorothy Rudledge. Middle row: John Blenkinsopp, Mary Hulbert, Derek Hawkins, Patricia Arnold, Michael Dunn, Barbara Hedges, Mac Summers, Mary Nicholls, David Biggin, Ann Phillips. Front row: Roland Rosser, Pauline Robson, Michael Teague, Mary Clutterbuck, Mr Rabley, Mr Rouch, Miss Cook, Michael Lewis, Joan Timbrell, Gerald Dicker, Patricia Harvey.

Opposite below: The school Photographic Society visit to Chepstow Castle, *c.* 1949. From left to right, back row: Catherine Skinner, Mr Hill, Peter Nott. Front row: Mr Peter Carpenter, -?-, -?-, Marian Thomas.

Left: A school expedition to the Mendips to go potholing, *c.* 1951. From left to right, back row: Eric Locke, John Cantrill. Second row: Don Malpass, -?-, Graham Adams, Michael Dunn. Third row: Barbara Hedges, John White, Wendy Artus, -?. Front: John Blenkinsopp (standing), Marjorie Beck.

Below: The headmaster and staff with clergy, *c.* 1948. From left to right, back row: -?-, Mr Johnson (PE), Mrs Timbrell, Mr Williams, Mr Pennington, Mr Harwood. Middle row: Miss Rees (Biology), Miss Smith (Commercial and French), Mrs Williams, Miss Cook (English), Miss Gale. Front row: Miss Nixon, -?-, Mr Rouch, Revd R. Rawstorne, Mrs Mair Johnson (*née* Jones).

Opposite above: The 1952 rugby team. From left to right, back row: Peter Wilson, -?-, John Lock, Roger Bennett, Roger Jackson. Middle row: Mr Pedlar, Alan Bain, John Lovell, Colin Tanner, Eric Hope, Doug Foster, Brindley Powell, Mr Gunn. Front row: Dennis Ewins, Brian Moorcroft, George Ford, Taff Williams, Francis Haydon, Alan Slade, Tony Iles.

The 1953/54 hockey team. Back row: Sylvia Smith, Pat Morley. Middle row: Mr Rouch, Betty Knapp, Ann Williams, Ann Codling, Maureen Chidgey, Miss Richardson. Front row: Sylvia Palmer, Josie Hurcombe, Captain Marion Davies, Margaret Wright, Mary McIntyre.

Left: Members of staff took a group of pupils on a ten-day geography trip to the Lake District in April 1952. From left to right, back row: Mr B.H. Cudmore (Geography), Mr Beynon (Maths). Middle row: Mr Ken Jenkins (Woodwork), Miss Mary Taylor (Geography), Miss Joan Richardson (History and PE), Miss Eileen Walker (Maths). Front row: Mr Copley (Music), Mr Trevor Wright (Latin).

Below: The cold, wet weather in the Lake District did not dampen the spirits of the group, although they do look seriously under-equipped by today's standards. From left to right, back row: Mr Wright, Brian Thompson, John Blenkinsopp, Bob Sharpe, Don Malpass, Judy Watkins, Graham Hannaford, John Smith, Patricia Arnold, Barbara Hedges, -?-, Miss Taylor, Mr Jenkins, Mr Beynon, Ian Jackson. Front row: Marion Davies, Valerie Harding, Eileen Powell, Elizabeth Nash, Christopher Woodward, Colin Radford.

A party of sixth formers and staff enjoyed a geography trip by Riddiford's coach to Scotland during Easter 1954. The school magazine describes an attempt to climb Ben Nevis, which was thwarted at around 4,000ft due to thick snow and ice. It also recorded one pupil's account of the trip back: 'We left Scotland by way of Carter Bar, where a thrilling race along the last quarter of a mile into England was followed by cheers at entering the Motherland, and much taking of photographs'.

A geography and biology trip to the Gower Peninsula, Easter 1960. From left to right, back row: Valerie Collier, -?-, -?-, Angela Oliver, Mr Lodge, Roger Bailey, -?-, -?-, Reg Riddiford (coachdriver). Middle row: Jill Knapp, Helen Haste, Marilyn Evans, Marguerite Copola, Jackie Raymond, Geraldine Starling, -?-, Miss Rees, Mary Thompson, Janice Daniels, Colin Burden, ? Watson. Front row: Vanessa Carey, Miss Cleverly, Richard Lodge (son of Mr Lodge), Margaret Davis.

The cricket First XI, *c.* 1953. From left to right, back row: Michael Ponting, Johnny Lovall, Leonard Griffiths, -?-, Tony Pritchard. Middle row: Mr Young, ? Watts, Brian Hobkirk, Don Exell, Colin Pawsey, Mr Gunn. Front row: John 'Ernie' Riddle, Don Malpass, Mr Rouch, Brian Thompson, Chris Woodward.

Howard House won the Old Thornburians' Athletics Shield, presented at Sports Day 1954. From left to right: House Captain Marion Davies, headmaster Mr Rouch, Sir Stanley Hooker of Rolls-Royce, Athletics Captain Keith Rowley.

A tennis group, *c.* 1957. From left to right, back row: Jill Knapp, Gloria Boxwell, Hilary Clark. Front row: Miss P. Cleverly, Ann Clark, Linda Manning, Mary Thompson, Mr Johnson.

The 1957 football team. From left to right, back row: Keith Marshall, Derek Morris. Middle row: Pete Wilson, Pat Hawkins, Andy Davies, Dave Thompson, Tony Harding, Mr Johnson. Front row: John Phillips, Alan Slade, Roger Jackson, Colin Tanner, Alan 'Ginger' Dickinson.

A tennis group, *c.* 1958. From left to right, back row: Jill Knapp, Miss M. Preston, Val Collier. Front row: Angela Oliver, –?–, Mary Thompson, Marguerite Capola.

The prefects, 1960. From left to right, back row: R. Entwhistle, Brian Prew, Geoffrey Rickards, –?–. Second row: Derek Rosser, Michael Gee, Peter Nellthorp, Roger Bayley, Susan Rees, Valerie Hargreaves, Angela Oliver, G. Bailey, David King, Colin Burden, P. Armstrong. Third row: Cynthia Rouse, Susan Rea, Patricia Weeks, Jacqueline Webber, Janice Daniels, Caris Jones, Hilary Clark, Vanessa Carey, Valerie Collier, Ruth White, Wendy Baker, Susan Newman. Front row: Alan Jenkins, Barbara Cole, Chester Riddiford, Frances Taylor, David Skuse, Miss Rees, Mr Rouch, Mr Hodge, Jill Knapp, Peter Wilcox,, Jeanne Pearce, David Burgess, Mary Thompson.

The junior cross-country race, 1959. The clock facing the playing field is a memorial to former pupils who were killed during the Second World War. Of the visible faces are, from left to right: -?-, C. Brown, R. Keating, I. Stanworth, Graham Smith, ? Cook, -?-, Richard Shaw, -?-, Peter Townsend, Bruce Davies, Phillip Jones, Clive Dunn, Geoff Wilson, Robert Stockley. The winner of the race was C. Brown.

Boys enjoying some time out of lessons, c. 1959. From left to right, back row: Don Mondus, Chris Doig, -?-, Alan Hayward. Middle row: -?-, -?-, Paul Gregory. Front row: -?-, Dave Greaves, ? Powell. Many Old Thornburians have fond memories of their time at Thornbury Grammar School.

Other local titles published by Tempus

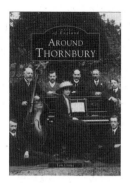

Around Thornbury

TOM CROWE

This selection of images captures the South Gloucestershire town of Thornbury and surrounding villages, including Olveston, Tytherington, Oldbury-on-Severn and Charfield during the last century. Illustrated with over 220 archive photographs and postcards gathered from private collections and the archive at Thornbury and District Museum, each picture provides an insight into a bygone way of life.

0 7524 2926 4

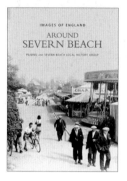

Around Severn Beach

PILNING AND SEVERN BEACH LOCAL HISTORY GROUP

This fascinating collection of over 200 archive pictures highlights some of the changes that have taken place in and around Severn Beach during the last century. Life in some of the surrounding villages is also recalled here, including Pilning, Redwick, Easter Compton, Almondsbury, Tockington and Elberton. This book is a valuable pictorial history which will reawaken nostalgic memories for some, while offering a unique glimpse of the past for others.

0 7524 3392 X

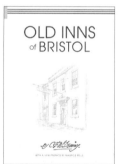

Old Inns of Bristol

C.F.W. DENING, WITH A NEW PREFACE BY MAURICE FELLS

Old Inns of Bristol is a fascinating guide to the historic pubs in the city. First published in 1943, the original book is reproduced here, along with an updated preface by local writer and broadcaster Maurice Fells. This book offers the reader an insight into the life of pubs past and present, from the oddly named Rhubarb Tavern to the dockside pubs with their stories of pirates and smugglers.

0 7524 3475 6

Haunted Bristol

SUE LE'QUEUX

This selection of newspaper reports and first-hand accounts recalls strange and spooky happenings in Bristol's ancient streets, churches, theatres and public houses. From paranormal manifestations at the Bristol Old Vic to the ghostly activity of a grey monk who is said to haunt Bristol's twelfth-century cathedral, this spine-tingling collection of supernatural tales is sure to appeal to anyone interested in Bristol's haunted heritage.

0 7524 3300 8

If you are interested in purchasing other books published by Tempus, or in case you have difficulty finding any Tempus books in your local bookshop, you can also place orders directly through our website

www.tempus-publishing.com